EASY TO COOK

HOT & SPICY

Hilaire Walden

ANAYA PUBLISHERS LTD
LONDON

First published in Great Britain in 1993 by
ANAYA PUBLISHERS LTD.
Strode House, 44-50 Osnaburgh Street, London NW1 3ND

Design and art direction by Patrick McLeavey & Partners, London

Photographer: Patrick McLeavey
Home Economist: Meg Jansz
Photographic Stylists: Sue Storey, Marian Price

British Library Cataloguing in Publication Data
Walden, Hilaire
Easy to cook hot & spicy. – (Easy to cook)

ISBN 1–85470–160–6

Typeset by Bookworm Typesetting, Manchester
Colour reproduction by Scantrans Pte Ltd, Singapore
Printed in Great Britain by Butler and Tanner Ltd, Frome and London

NOTES
Ingredients are listed in metric, imperial and cup
measurements.
Use one set of quantities as they are not
interchangeable.

All spoon measures are level:
1 tablespoon = one 15ml spoon
1 teaspoon = one 5ml spoon.

Use fresh herbs and freshly ground black pepper
unless otherwise stated.

Use standard size 3 eggs unless otherwise
suggested.

Throughout this book 'Preparation time' refers to the time required
to prepare the ingredients. It does not include time for cooking,
soaking, marinading etc, which is given in the recipe method.

CONTENTS

In recent years there has been more and more emphasis on food that requires relatively little time to prepare. At the same time there has been a renewed awareness of the wide range of spices and flavourings available to the modern cook. Happily, these two trends can go hand in hand, so there is no reason why fast food should be lacking in flavour. Quite the reverse in fact, as there is now a widespread acceptance of more strongly flavoured dishes.

The recipes in this book are drawn from all parts of the world, and have been included for their intrinsic flavour, as well as 'hotness'. You will also find recipes which make a virtue of combining unusual ingredients from different cuisines. The common element in all these dishes is, of course, the wonderful range of exotic herbs, spices and flavourings which will add life to any meal.

These ingredients will inspire your everyday cooking and are invaluable when entertaining, especially if you want to create dishes that are a little out of the ordinary. There are so many varieties to choose from, all suitable for using individually, or in a wide range of fascinating combinations. Herbs and spices are quick and easy to use: many can simply be rubbed into pieces of fish or meat, while others can be added to marinades, or used as flavourings in stews or casseroles. You can add them to salad dressings, rice and pasta, or even to desserts and drinks.

Although they are quick to prepare, the taste of many spiced dishes will improve with time, because the flavours become more mellow. So, when a recipe calls for ingredients to be marinated, do try to leave the dish for the time specified. It is worth bearing in mind that smaller pieces of food will be flavoured by a marinade more quickly than large ones, and that the food will absorb the flavour more quickly at room temperature than, say, in a refrigerator. The flavour of such dishes as casseroles, sauces and salad dressings will also benefit from being made a day in advance. The list that follows will give you a guide to the basic spices and flavourings, but it is by no means exhaustive.

HOT INGREDIENTS

Cayenne pepper: a fiercely hot, fine powder made from certain chillies.

Chillies: chillies add a distinct flavour as well as 'hotness' to dishes. There are many different varieties of chilli, all with their own taste and degree of 'hotness'. If you are unable to get the colour or type of chilli mentioned in a recipe don't abandon the recipe altogether, but try to use what is available, bearing in mind that large chillies are milder than small ones. Red chillies are ripened green chillies, so they have a sweeter taste than the fresh, crisp 'green' note of the immature form. Dried chillies have a more earthy, fruity flavour, which can be enhanced by roasting. Fresh chillies can be treated in a similar manner.

The seeds and veins of chillies are hotter than the flesh, have less flavour, and are generally removed and discarded. However, if you really like very hot dishes, you can leave them in. Chillies contain an oil which can irritate the eyes and skin, so when you are handling them make sure that any cuts or bruises are covered and avoid touching the eyes and mouth. Always wash your hands after preparing chillies, or to be completely safe, wear rubber gloves.

Chilli pepper flakes: also known as 'hot red pepper flakes', these are milder than whole dried chillies.

Chilli powder: in Britain this will have been made from ground chillies, and is hot, but American chilli powders will also contain ground herbs and other spices, and may be milder as a result. To be sure of the strength of the powder check the contents label.

Ginger: the fresh root has a warm, sweetish aroma, but its flavour is hot and slightly biting.

Harissa: this is a fiery North African sauce, used in cooking and also as a table condiment. It can be bought ready-made in small cans, but it is easy to make. The basic ingredients are dried chillies, garlic, cumin and caraway seeds, dried mint, olive oil and salt.

Horseradish: freshly grated horseradish has a flavour and aroma so pungent that it can provoke tears. 'Prepared horseradish' is grated horseradish preserved in vinegar, and is the strongest ready prepared product.

Mustard: English and Chinese mustards are hotter, but have less flavour than the French types. German and American types are usually the mildest. The flavour of all mustards tends to lessen when they are heated, so for maximum effect, add mustard towards the end of the cooking.

Pepper: white pepper has a hotter taste than the black variety, but is less aromatic. Green peppercorns are not as hot as white or black, and have a fresh, almost sharp flavour.

Wasabi: this comes from a horseradish-type root and is used in Japanese cuisine. It is sold dried or as a green paste, and is very fiery, so use it in moderation.

COCONUT MILK

This is not the liquid found at the centre of the hollow nut, but is a type of juice extracted from the surrounding flesh. Coconut milk is available in cans (which affects the flavour slightly) and in plastic pouches. However it can be easily prepared at home, from creamed coconut or unsweetened dessicated coconut, and will keep in the refrigerator. If you are using creamed coconut, simply dissolve 150 g (5 oz) of the material in a jug of hot water (about 300 ml or 10 fl oz). For dessicated coconut, allow 225 g (8 oz) of coconut and 300 ml (10 fl oz) of boiling water, and leave the mixture to steep for about 30 minutes.

Transfer the mixture to a food processor and blend for about 1 minute. Tip the mixture into a sieve lined with muslin and squeeze the cloth hard to extract as much liquid as possible.

BUYING INGREDIENTS

It is best to buy spices from a shop which has a good turnover; this applies equally to supermarkets and specialist or ethnic shops. Purchase both dried and fresh ingredients in amounts that you will use quite quickly, as flavours deteriorate over time. The flavour should be quite acceptable for 4-6 months in the case of ground spices, and up to 8 months for whole ones, providing that the product has been stored correctly.

STORAGE

Fresh chillies, ginger and lemon grass will keep for up to 2 weeks if loosely wrapped in paper towels, placed in a plastic bag and stored in a cool place, or in the salad drawer of the refrigerator. Dried spices are best stored in glass jars with tight fitting lids, or other inert containers that can be made airtight. Store them in a cool, dark place. It is a good idea to label the containers with the date of purchase so that you can keep a check on their age.

DRY ROASTING

To bring out the flavour and aroma of whole dry spices dry roast, or toast them, before grinding them, or incorporating them into a dish. Heat a heavy frying pan, add the whole spices, and place the pan over a medium heat for several minutes. Shake the pan frequently, to prevent burning, and continue until a fragrant aroma is given off.

GRINDING AND CRUSHING SPICES

Ground spices lose their aroma and flavour more quickly than whole spices, so whenever possible, grind them near to the time when they are required. Most whole spices are easy to grind, the exceptions being cinnamon, mace and turmeric. Traditionally, a pestle and mortar are used, although the end of a rolling pin in a bowl can mimic the action. The process, however, can be a little laborious. If you grind spices frequently it is worth buying an electric grinder, a coffee grinder or a small blender to use specifically for grinding spices. A peppermill works well for seeds and berries such as allspice and coriander.

Sometimes spices just need to be lightly crushed in order to release the flavour. To do this, either press the spice with a pestle in a mortar, or place the spice in an envelope or bag and roll or tap the contents with a rolling pin.

FRESH SPICES

Some spices, such as ginger root and lemon grass, are available fresh. To prepare fresh ginger, peel off the brown skin using a vegetable peeler or small knife. The required amount can then be grated from the root, or cut off in slices. To chop ginger, crush it first with the flat side of the knife, to loosen the fibres, then chop finely. With lemon grass, peel away the outer layer and cut off and discard the root end and the upper part of the stem. Unless you specially require the whole piece, lemon grass should be chopped very finely across the stem, or else made into a paste.

INGREDIENTS

3 hot green chillies, chopped
4 ripe tomatoes, peeled, seeded and
  chopped
55 g (2 oz) coriander (cilantro)
  leaves
2 cloves garlic
1 small onion, chopped
juice of 1 lime
salt

METHOD

Preparation time: 5 minutes

Put all the ingredients into a blender or food processor.

Switch the motor on and off, or use a pulse action, to mix the ingredients to a knobbly texture.

Pour into a bowl and add salt to taste. Cover and leave for 1-2 hours before serving in tacos or with fish, seafood, grilled poultry or meat, or salads.

Makes 300-350 ml (10-12 fl oz/1¼- 1½ cups)

INGREDIENTS

25 g (1 oz) coriander seeds
20 g (³/₄ oz) cardamom seeds
25 g (1 oz) cumin seeds
2 cinnamon sticks, broken
20 g (³/₄ oz) black peppercorns
15 g (½ oz) whole cloves
2 bay leaves, crumbled
15 g (½ oz) ground mace

METHOD

Preparation time: 5 minutes

Heat a heavy frying pan. Add all the ingredients except the mace, and leave over a medium heat until the spices become fragrant and darken in colour, shaking the pan frequently to prevent them burning.

Tip into a mortar or small blender and add the mace. Leave to cool.

Pound together until finely ground. Store in an airtight jar for up to 3 months.

Makes about 125 g (4½ oz)

INGREDIENTS

2 dried red chillies
2 teaspoons coriander seeds
2 teaspoons cumin seeds
1 teaspoon mustard seeds
1 teaspoon cardamom seeds
8 cloves
7.5 cm (3 in) cinnamon stick, broken
1 teaspoon ground ginger
1 teaspoon ground turmeric

METHOD

Preparation time: 5 minutes

Heat a heavy frying pan. Add the chillies, coriander, cumin, mustard and cardamom seeds, cloves and cinnamon. Leave, shaking the pan frequently, until darkened, but do not allow the spices to burn.

Leave to cool, then tip into a small blender or mortar and crush to a powder.

Add the ginger and turmeric and mix thoroughly. Store in an airtight jar in a cool, dark place for up to 3 months.

Makes about 3 tablespoons

INGREDIENTS

about 22 whole dried shrimps,
  chopped
3 cloves garlic, chopped
4 dried red chillies with seeds,
  chopped
1 tablespoon fish sauce
2 tablespoons lime juice
1 fresh red or green chilli, chopped

METHOD   Preparation time: 5 minutes

Put the shrimps, garlic, dried chillies, fish sauce and lime juice into a mortar or small blender and pound to a paste.

Transfer the paste to a small serving bowl. Stir in the chopped fresh chilli.

Store in an airtight jar in the refrigerator for several weeks. Serve with a selection of raw vegetables.

Serves 6-8

INGREDIENTS

1 tablespoon coriander seeds
1 teaspoon cumin seeds
1 teaspoon black peppercorns
4 cloves garlic, chopped
3 coriander roots, chopped
8 dried red chillies, seeded and
  chopped
2 stalks lemon grass, chopped
grated rind of ½ kaffir lime
3 cm (1½ in) galangal, chopped
2 teaspoons shrimp paste

METHOD

Preparation time: 5 minutes

Heat a wok, add the coriander and cumin seeds and heat until the seeds become fragrant.

Tip the seeds into a mortar or small blender and crush with the peppercorns.

Add the remaining ingredients and pound to a smooth paste. Store in an airtight jar in the refrigerator.

Makes about 4 tablespoons

Note: The yield and hotness will vary according to the size and heat of the chillies.

INGREDIENTS

4 tablespoons vegetable oil
8 fresh red chillies, thinly sliced
8 fresh green chillies, thinly sliced
2 large onions, thinly sliced
4 cloves garlic, thinly sliced
2 carrots, chopped
1 red pepper (capsicum), sliced
1 teaspoon oregano
1 teaspoon marjoram
1 teaspoon thyme
750 ml (20 fl oz/2½ cups) distilled
  white vinegar
1 tablespoon sugar
salt and freshly ground black pepper

METHOD   **Preparation time:** 10 minutes

Heat the oil in a saucepan, add the chillies and sauté for 2 minutes. Transfer to a bowl. Repeat with the onions and garlic, then the carrots, and lastly the red pepper (capsicum).

Add the herbs to the pan, remove from the heat and pour in the vinegar. Add the sugar and seasonings, return to the heat and stir until the sugar has dissolved. Bring to the boil and boil until the liquid reduces by one-third.

Pour the liquid over the vegetables, stir and leave to cool. Transfer to sterilized jars and seal tightly. Store for 1 month before serving as an accompaniment, especially to meat and cheese dishes, or in sandwiches, tacos or tortillas. Refrigerate after opening.

Makes about 1.2 litres (2 pints/5 cups)

INGREDIENTS

20-25 dried small red chillies
3 tablespoons oil
4 shallots, chopped
4 cloves garlic, chopped
juice of 3-4 limes
1 teaspoon sugar
2 tablespoons fish sauce

METHOD

Preparation time: 10 minutes

Soak the chillies in hot water until soft. Drain, Heat the oil in a frying pan, add the chillies, shallots and garlic and fry for 4-5 minutes, stirring.

Remove the pan from the heat, cool briefly, then tip the contents into a blender. Add the lime juice, sugar and fish sauce and mix until smooth.

Adjust amounts of lime juice and sugar, if necessary, then transfer to a dish or jar. Cool completely, then cover and keep for at least 2 hours before serving, or store in an airtight jar in the refrigerator for up to 2 weeks.

Makes about 300 g (10 oz/1¼ cups)

INGREDIENTS

3 cloves garlic, unpeeled
225 g (8 oz) beefsteak tomatoes
1 red pepper (capsicum)
25 g (1 oz) blanched almonds
1 dried hot red chilli, soaked in cold
* water for 30 minutes, drained and*
* seeded*
3 tablespoons red wine vinegar
about 150 ml (¼ pint/⅔ cup) olive
* oil*
salt

METHOD   Preparation time: 5 minutes

Preheat the oven to its hottest setting. Put the garlic, tomatoes and red pepper (capsicum) on a baking tray and bake for 20-30 minutes, removing the tomatoes and garlic when soft and the pepper when soft and lightly browned. Add the almonds to the vegetables for about 5 minutes until lightly browned.

Peel the tomatoes and red pepper and discard the seeds. Peel the garlic. Mix the vegetables, almonds and chilli in a food processor or blender; then, with the motor running, pour in the vinegar slowly with enough oil to make a thick sauce.

Add salt to taste. Leave to stand for 3-4 hours before serving with meat, fish or vegetable dishes.

Serves 6

– 1 –
SNACKS AND FIRST COURSES

INGREDIENTS

3 tablespoons olive oil
4 tablespoons sesame seeds
115 g (4 oz/1 cup) skinned hazelnuts
115 g (4 oz/1 cup) cashew nuts
115 g (4 oz/1 cup) unblanched
  almonds
salt
2 teaspoons Worcestershire sauce
2 teaspoons curry powder
1 teaspoon chilli powder
coarse salt

METHOD   Preparation time: 5 minutes

Heat the oil in a frying pan, add the sesame seeds, hazelnuts and cashew nuts and fry, stirring occasionally, until lightly browned.

Stir in the almonds for about 30 seconds, then stir in the Worcestershire sauce, curry powder and chilli powder.

Cook for 2-3 minutes, stirring frequently, then tip into a bowl, sprinkle with salt and leave to cool. Serve with drinks or as a snack.

Makes about 400g (14 oz)

INGREDIENTS

800 g (1¾ lb) large green olives
3 dried red chillies
4 cloves garlic
long strip of lemon peel
3 sprigs dill
3 sprigs thyme
3 sprigs oregano
2 teaspoons fennel seeds
olive oil

METHOD   Preparation time: 10 minutes

With the point of a sharp knife, cut a slit in each olive through to the stone (pit).

Layer the olives with the chillies, garlic cloves, lemon peel, herb sprigs and fennel seeds in a large jar.

Pour in sufficient oil to cover, then close the jar and leave for 1 month before using. Serve with drinks, as an appetizer or in salads; use the oil for cooking.

Makes 800 g (1¾ lb)

INGREDIENTS

85 g (3 oz/¾ cup) chick-pea flour, sifted
1 teaspoon ground cumin seeds
1 teaspoon ground coriander seeds
large pinch of baking powder
salt
2 fresh green chillies, finely chopped
125 ml (4 fl oz/½ cup) warm water
2 teaspoons peanut oil (plus extra for deep-frying)
2 onions, thinly sliced into rings

METHOD   Preparation time: 10 minutes

Stir the flour, cumin, coriander, baking powder, salt and chillies together in a large bowl. Form a well in the centre of the mixture, then slowly pour in the water and oil, whisking constantly with a wire whisk. Alternatively, this can be done in a food processor.

Half-fill a deep-fat fryer with oil and heat to 190° C (375° F). Stir the onions into the batter. Lower about five portions of batter into the oil, taking care not to overcrowd the pan. Reduce the heat to 150° C (300° F) and continue to cook, turning the fritters occasionally until they are evenly browned, crisp on the outside and soft on the inside. This should take 8-10 minutes.

Using a slotted spoon, transfer the fritters to paper towels and allow to drain. Reheat the oil and cook the remaining batter in the same way. Serve hot.

Serves 4

INGREDIENTS

1 onion, quartered
400 g (14 oz) can chick-peas, drained
4 small dried red chillies, seeded
115 g (4 oz/2 cups) fresh
  breadcrumbs
¼ teaspoon cumin seeds
1 egg
3-4 cloves garlic
salt and freshly ground black pepper
1¼ tablespoons chopped coriander
  (cilantro)
seasoned flour for coating
about 5 tablespoons lemon juice
100 ml (3½ fl oz/scant ½ cup) tahini
100 ml (3½ fl oz/scant ½ cup) plain
  yogurt
black pepper
vegetable oil for deep-frying
coriander (cilantro) sprigs, for garnish

METHOD   Preparation time: 15 minutes

Put the onion, chick-peas, chillies, breadcrumbs, cumin, egg, 2 garlic cloves and salt into a food processor and blend until smooth. Add the chopped coriander (cilantro) and blend briefly.

Sprinkle your hands with seasoned flour, then form the chick-pea mixture into small balls. Set aside. In a blender, chop 1-2 cloves garlic with a little salt, add the lemon juice, tahini, yogurt and pepper and mix to a smooth cream, adding cold water if necessary. Adjust the lemon juice and seasoning, if necessary. Pour into a bowl.

Half-fill a deep-fat fryer with oil and heat to 190° C (375° F). Add some chick-pea balls and fry for about 3 minutes, until golden. Using a slotted spoon, transfer to paper towels to drain. Keep warm while frying the remaining mixture. Serve hot with the tahini dip, garnished with coriander sprigs.

Serves 4

INGREDIENTS

450 g (1 lb) uncooked medium
  prawns (shrimp) in their shells
2 teaspoons wasabi powder
4 tablespoons mayonnaise
2 teaspoons rice wine vinegar
salt
selection of lettuce leaves
½ avocado
1 tomato, skinned, seeded and
  chopped
1 small red onion, finely chopped
2 tablespoons chopped coriander
  (cilantro)

METHOD   Preparation time: 10 minutes

Add the prawns (shrimp) to a large saucepan of boiling water, bring back to the boil and cook until the shells turn pink (about 30 seconds). Drain and remove all the shells. Then, using the point of a sharp knife, cut along the back of each prawn and remove the dark thread. Cut the prawns into large chunks.

In a small bowl, mix together the wasabi powder and a small amount of water. Cover and leave for 5 minutes. Stir in the mayonnaise, vinegar and salt. Arrange the lettuce leaves in a shallow bowl or on a large plate.

Remove the stone (pit) from the avocado, then peel the avocado and cut into cubes. Toss with the prawns, tomato, red onions and coriander (cilantro) and moisten with the wasabi mayonnaise. Top the lettuce with the avocado mixture. Serve any remaining mayonnaise separately.

Serves 4

INGREDIENTS

700 g (1½ lb) fish fillets, such as
  plaice
1 tablespoon lemon juice
4 fresh green chillies
75 g (3 oz) coriander seeds
3 cloves garlic
225 ml (8 fl oz/1 cup) strained
  yogurt
salt
vegetable oil, for deep frying
coriander (cilantro) sprigs and lemon
  wedges, to serve

METHOD

Preparation time: 15 minutes

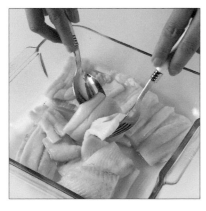

Cut the fish fillets into strips
approximately 4 x 6.5 cm (1½ x 2½
in) and place in a shallow dish.
Sprinkle with the lemon juice and turn
the fish strips to coat them evenly.

Mix the chillies, coriander and garlic
to a paste with 2-3 tablespoons of the
yogurt in a food processor. Add the
remaining yogurt and salt, spoon over
the fish, turning the strips to coat
them evenly, cover and leave for 1
hour, turning two or three times.

Remove the fish from the yogurt
mixture. Heat the oil in a deep fat-
fryer to 180°C (350°F) and deep-fry
the fish in batches for 2-3 minutes
until evenly browned. Remove using a
slotted spoon and drain on paper
towels. Serve hot with coriander
(cilantro) sprigs and lemon wedges.

Serves 4

INGREDIENTS

2 cloves garlic
250 ml (8 fl oz/1 cup) mayonnaise
½ teaspoon wholegrain mustard
½ teaspoon paprika
1 tablespoon freshly grated
  Parmesan cheese
¼ red pepper (capsicum), chopped
3 spring onions (scallions), including
  some green, chopped
1 ½ teaspoons Worcestershire sauce
few drops of Tabasco sauce
1 tablespoon horseradish sauce
450 g (1 lb) crab meat

METHOD   Preparation time: 10 minutes

Drop the garlic into a food processor or blender, with the motor running.

Stop the motor and add the remaining ingredients, except the crab meat. Blend until combined.

Transfer the mixture to a bowl, stir in the crab meat, then cover and chill. Serve with sticks of raw vegetables such as celery, carrot and cucumber, and cauliflower florets.

Serves 6-8

CEVICHE

INGREDIENTS

450 g (1 lb) fresh, firm-fleshed white fish, such as haddock, cod or monkfish
juice of 4 limes
2-3 fresh green chillies, finely chopped
½ small red onion, sliced and separated into rings
2-3 tablespoons olive oil
1 small red pepper (capsicum), finely chopped
3 ripe but firm tomatoes, skinned, seeded and finely chopped
salt
leaves from several coriander (cilantro) sprigs, chopped

METHOD

Preparation time: 15 minutes

Using a sharp knife, cut the fish into thin slices. Lay the slices in a shallow, non-metallic dish, pour over the lime juice, scatter with the chillies, cover and leave at room temperature for 1 hour, or chill for 2-4 hours, turning occasionally.

Drain the lime juice from the fish and mix with the oil, pepper (capsicum), tomato and salt.

Pour over the fish, sprinkle with the coriander (cilantro), cover again and chill for 30 minutes.

Serves 4

INGREDIENTS

2 tablespoons olive oil
2 onions, finely chopped
2 cloves garlic, crushed
8 slices smoked back bacon, chopped
1 teaspoon chilli powder
1 teaspoon ground roasted cumin
400 g (14 oz) can red kidney beans
*575 g (1¼ lb) canned chopped
  tomatoes*
1 tablespoon tomato pureé (paste)
salt and freshly ground black pepper
8 taco shells
1 ripe avocado
juice of 1 lime
*soured cream and black olives, to
  serve*

METHOD   Preparation time: 15 minutes

Heat the oil in a saucepan. Add the onion, garlic and bacon and cook, stirring occasionally, for 4 minutes. Add the chilli powder and cumin and stir for 1-2 minutes.

Drain and rinse the kidney beans, then add to the pan with the tomatoes, tomato pureé (paste) and salt and pepper. Cover and simmer for 15 minutes, stirring occasionally. Heat the taco shells according to the instructions on the packet.

Cut the avocado in half lengthways, remove the stone (pit), and slice the flesh; reserve 8 slices and sprinkle these with lime juice. Chop the remaining slices and add to pan. Heat for 1-2 minutes, stirring occasionally. Divide the bean mixture between the tacos, add 1 tablespoon soured cream to the centre of each and top with an avocado slice and black olive.

Serves 4

INGREDIENTS

oil for deep-frying
6 tortillas
55 g (2 oz/½ cup) Cheddar cheese,
* grated*
25 g (1 oz/¼ cup) mozzarella cheese,
* grated*
1 onion, finely chopped
1 green pepper (capsicum), finely
* chopped*
1 green chilli, finely chopped
150 ml (¼ pint/⅔ cup) soured cream
coriander (cilantro) leaves and chilli
* pepper flakes, to serve*

METHOD

Preparation time: 15 minutes

Heat the oil in a deep-fat fryer to 180° C (350° F). Meanwhile, stack the tortillas and cut into 8 pieces. Place about one-third in the frying basket, lower into the oil and fry, shaking the basket, until just golden and crisp (about 2 minutes). Drain on paper towels while frying the remaining pieces in the same way.

Preheat the grill. Spread the nachos in a single layer on baking trays. Mix the cheeses and put on to the nachos. Mix the onion, green pepper (capsicum) and chilli and sprinkle over the cheese.

Grill the nachos until the cheese melts, then top with a little soured cream and sprinkle with coriander (cilantro) leaves and chilli pepper flakes. Serve immediately.

Serves 6

INGREDIENTS

115 g (4 oz) soft cheese
2 spring onions (scallions), white
*   part only, finely chopped*
1 garlic clove, finely chopped
55 g (2 oz) ham, minced
1½ teaspoons chopped mixed herbs
salt
4 tablespoons virgin olive oil
1 tablespoon lime juice
1 tablespoon chopped coriander
*   (cilantro)*
6 fresh red chillies
6 fresh green chillies

METHOD   Preparation time: 15 minutes

Preheat the grill. Mix together the cheese, spring onions (scallions), garlic, ham, herbs and salt; set aside. Stir together the oil, lime juice and coriander (cilantro); set aside.

Grill the chillies, turning occasionally, until evenly charred. Leave until cool enough to handle, then scrape off the skin. Cut in half lengthways, remove the cores and seeds.

Divide the cheese mixture between the chillies and arrange on a serving plate. Spoon the oil mixture over the filling and leave in a cool place, not the refrigerator, for 2 hours.

Serves 4-6

INGREDIENTS

2 teaspoons plain (all-purpose) flour
½ teaspoon dry English mustard
½ teaspoon dried herbes de Provence
freshly ground black pepper
4 Camembert portions, about 40 g
  (1½ oz) each
about 25 g (1 oz/¼ cup) dry
  breadcrumbs
about 25 g (1 oz/¼ cup) sesame
  seeds
1 teaspoon paprika
about ¼ teaspoon cayenne pepper
1 egg, beaten
vegetable oil for deep-frying

METHOD

Preparation time: 10 minutes

Mix together the flour, mustard, herbs and black pepper. Rub evenly over the cheese portions. Cover and chill for at least 4 hours, or put in the freezer for 1 hour.

Mix together the breadcrumbs, sesame seeds, paprika and cayenne pepper to taste.

Dip the cheese portions in the beaten egg, allow the excess to drain off, then coat evenly in the breadcrumb mixture, pressing it on firmly. Half-fill a deep-fat fryer with oil and heat to 190° C (375° F). Fry the cheese portions for about 30 seconds until golden. Using a slotted spoon, transfer to paper towels to drain. Serve hot.

Serves 4

DEVILLED KIDNEYS

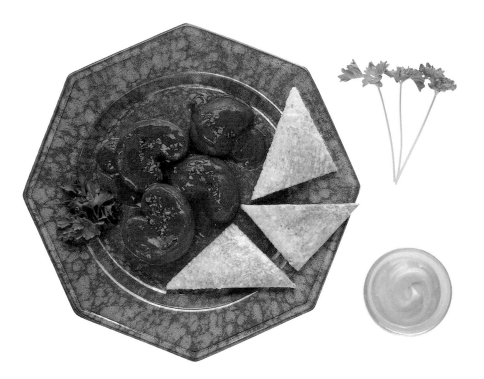

INGREDIENTS

2 teaspoons Worcestershire sauce
1 tablespoon tomato pureé (paste)
1 tablespoon lemon juice
1 tablespoon prepared English
  mustard
salt and cayenne pepper
40 g (1½ oz/1½ tablespoons)
  unsalted butter
225 g (8 oz) lambs' kidneys, skinned,
  halved and cores removed
1 tablespoon chopped parsley, for
  garnish
hot buttered toast, to serve

METHOD

Preparation time: 10 minutes

Mix together the Worcestershire sauce, tomato purée (paste), lemon juice and mustard. Add salt and cayenne pepper to taste.

Melt the butter in a frying pan, add the kidneys and cook over a medium heat for 3 minutes on each side.

Pour the mustard mixture over and stir quickly to coat the kidneys. Sprinkle with the chopped parsley and serve immediately with hot buttered toast.

Serves 2-3

INGREDIENTS

2 tablespoons olive oil
1 clove garlic, crushed
2 red peppers (capsicums), seeded
  and sliced
2 onions, thinly sliced
4 small spicy sausages, sliced
1½ tablespoons caraway seeds,
  crushed
1½ tablespoons paprika
4 large tomatoes, skinned and
  quartered
1-2 teaspoons harissa
salt
4 eggs

METHOD

Preparation time: 15 minutes

Heat the oil in a frying pan, add the garlic, peppers and onions and sauté until almost soft. Add the sausages and fry for about 3 minutes.

Stir in the caraway seeds, paprika, tomatoes, harissa and salt. Cook gently for 8-10 minutes, stirring occasionally, until the mixture thickens.

Adjust the seasoning of the red pepper (capsicum) mixture, if necessary. Make 4 indentations in the mixture, break an egg into each one, cover the pan and cook gently until the eggs are cooked to the required degree.

Serves 4

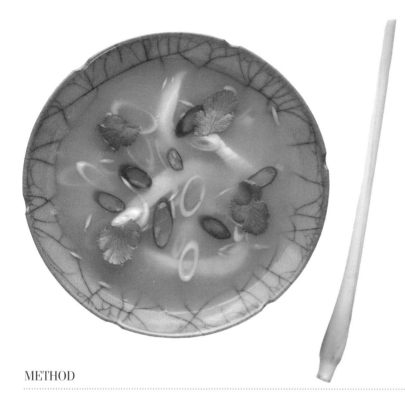

INGREDIENTS

175-225 g (6-8 oz) chicken breast
600 ml (1 pint/2½ cups) chicken
  stock
2 fat stalks lemon grass, finely
  chopped
3 tablespoons lime juice
1 tablespoon fish sauce
1¼ tablespoons grated lime zest
½ fresh red chilli, thinly sliced
½ fresh green chilli, thinly sliced
pinch of sugar
coriander (cilantro) leaves, to
  garnish

METHOD   Preparation time: 10 minutes

Cut the chicken across the grain into thin strips. Pour the stock into a saucepan with the lemon grass, lime juice, fish sauce, lime zest, chillies and sugar. Simmer for 5 minutes.

Add the chicken strips and cook at just below simmering point for 2-3 minutes until they are cooked.

Serve the soup in hot bowls garnished with coriander (cilantro) leaves.

Serves 4

– 2–
FISH AND SHELLFISH

INGREDIENTS

12 scallops on the half shell
1 tablespoon vegetable oil
2 cloves garlic, chopped
1 shallot, finely chopped
5 mm (¼ in) fresh ginger root, finely chopped
1½ teaspoons finely chopped fresh rcd chilli
freshly ground black pepper
3 tablespoons lime juice
¼ teaspoon sugar
1 teaspoon fish sauce
shredded coriander (cilantro) leaves, to garnish

METHOD   Preparation time: 10 minutes

Place the scallops on their shells in a steaming basket. Heat the oil in a frying pan, add the garlic and shallot and cook, stirring occasionally, until softened. Add the ginger and chilli, stir for 1 minute. Sprinkle over the scallops in the steaming basket and season with black pepper. Cover, place over a saucepan of boiling water and steam for 6-8 minutes until the scallops just begin to turn opaque.

In a small saucepan, gently heat the lime juice, sugar and fish sauce until the sugar dissolves.

Transfer the scallops on their shells to a serving plate, spoon over lime sauce and scatter coriander (cilantro) on top. Serve immediately.

Serves 3-4

INGREDIENTS

450 g (1 lb) uncooked large prawns
  (shrimp)
1 teaspoon roasted Sichuan
  peppercorns, ground
1½ teaspoons sea salt
3-4 teaspoons sugar
3 cloves garlic, finely chopped
1½ teaspoons fresh, ginger root,
  finely chopped
4 spring onions (scallions), chopped
2 fresh red chillies, chopped
175 ml (6 fl oz/¾ cup) groundnut oil

METHOD

Preparation time: 10 minutes

Remove the feathery legs of the prawns (shrimp), but do not remove the shells. Combine the peppercorns, salt and sugar in a small bowl. In a separate bowl combine the garlic, ginger, spring onions (scallions) and chillies.

Heat a wok or deep frying pan, add the oil and heat until very hot. Add the prawns and fry for 2-3 minutes. Using a slotted spoon, transfer the prawns to paper towels.

Drain the oil from the pan, leaving about 1 tablespoon. Stir in the peppercorn mixture, stir-fry for 10 seconds, then add the chilli mixture and stir-fry for 2 minutes. Return the prawns to the pan and cook briskly for 1½-2 minutes until the shells are well coated with spice mixture. Serve immediately.

Serves 4

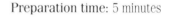

INGREDIENTS

4 thick cod steaks, about 200 g
  (7 oz) each
Marinade:
2 tablespoons roasted coriander
  seeds
1 tablespoon roasted cumin seeds
150 ml (¼ pint/⅔ cup) thick plain
  yogurt
1 teaspoon paprika
2 teaspoons dried dill
2 tablespoons chopped mint
2 large spring onions (scallions)
  chopped
2 cloves garlic, crushed
salt and freshly ground black pepper

METHOD

Preparation time: 5 minutes

Put all the marinade ingredients in a blender and mix to a paste.

Arrange the fish in a layer in a shallow flameproof dish. Spread the marinade evenly over the fish and leave in a cool place for 2-3 hours.

Preheat the grill. Put the fish under the grill and cook, basting occasionally until the fish flakes easily with the point of a knife, and the yogurt mixture has formed a crust (about 10-12 minutes). Serve immediately.

Serves 4

INGREDIENTS

2 tablespoons olive oil
1 onion, thinly sliced
2 cloves garlic, crushed
1 large fresh red chilli, finely chopped
5 cm (2 in) lemon grass, finely
  chopped
5 cm (2 in) fresh ginger root, finely
  chopped
2 tablespoons light soy sauce
2 tablespoons white wine vinegar
125 ml (4 fl oz/ ½ cup) water
about 3 tablespoons lime juice
6 salmon fillets, 115 g (4 oz) each
salt
2 medium mangoes
mixed salad leaves
12-14 mint leaves

METHOD

Preparation time: 20 minutes

Heat the oil in a large frying pan and stir in the onion, garlic, chilli, lemon grass and ginger. Continue to stir for 2 minutes. Add the soy sauce, vinegar, water and about 1 tablespoon lime juice. Simmer for 2 minutes, add the salmon and simmer gently for 3-4 minutes, turning the fish once. Add salt, if necessary, and more lime juice to taste. Remove the pan from heat and leave to cool.

Peel the mangoes, cut the flesh into thin strips and sprinkle with 1 tablespoon lime juice. Line a serving plate with lettuce leaves and scatter over the mango strips.

Place the salmon on the mango strips and scatter the mint leaves on top. Pour the cooking juices over the fish, cover the plate loosely with clingfilm and chill. Remove from the refrigerator about 10 minutes before serving.

Serves 6

INGREDIENTS

*½ teaspoon finely crushed cumin
  seeds*
1 teaspoon chilli powder
salt and freshly ground black pepper
2 tablespoons olive oil
2 cloves garlic, crushed
*1.25 cm (½ in) fresh ginger root,
  fincly chopped*
4 pieces salmon fillet, skinned
*125 ml (4 fl oz/½ cup) double
  (heavy) cream*
*250 ml (8 fl oz/1 cup) thick plain
  yogurt*
*large pinch of saffron threads,
  toasted and crushed*
*seeds from 6 cardamom pods,
  toasted and finely crushed*
salt
coriander (cilantro), to garnish

METHOD

Preparation time: 15 minutes

Mix together the cumin seeds, chilli powder and pepper and rub into the fish. Heat the oil in a frying pan, add the garlic and ginger and heat until they sizzle. Add the salmon fillets and fry until they start to colour (about 15-20 seconds on each side).

Stir in the cream, yogurt, saffron, cardamom and salt. Adjust the heat so that the sauce is just bubbling and cook, turning the fish once, until the flesh just flakes when tested with the point of a sharp knife (about 3-4 minutes each side).

Transfer the fish to a shallow dish. Boil the sauce until it has reduced and thickened, pour over the fish and leave to cool. Cover the dish and chill until 15-20 minutes before serving. Garnish with coriander (cilantro).

Serves 4

INGREDIENTS

700 g (1½ lb) skinned monkfish fillet
lime juice
salt and freshly ground black pepper
1 tablespoon vegetable oil
1 fresh green chilli, finely chopped
3 cloves garlic, finely crushed
1.25 cm (½ in) fresh ginger root,
  finely chopped
1 tablespoon finely crushed coriander
  seeds
2 teaspoons Garam Masala (see
  page 8)
150 ml (¼ pint/⅔ cup) plain yogurt
1 spring onion (scallion), finely
  chopped
lime wedges, to serve

METHOD

Preparation time: 15 minutes

Cut the monkfish into 2.5 cm (1 in) cubes and divide between four skewers. Lay in a shallow, non-metallic dish and sprinkle evenly with lime juice and pepper.

Heat the oil in a small frying pan, add the chilli, garlic and ginger and cook, stirring occasionally, for about 2 minutes. Stir in the coriander and heat for 2-3 minutes. Stir in the garam masala, heat briefly, then remove the pan from the heat and stir in the yogurt, spring onion (scallion) and salt. Cool slightly, then pour over fish, turning the skewers to coat the fish evenly. Cover and leave in a cool place for 2-3 hours.

Preheat the grill. Grill the kebabs, turning and basting occasionally with the yogurt mixture, for 3-4 minutes on each side until the flesh flakes easily when tested with the point of a knife. Serve with lime wedges.

Serves 4

37

INGREDIENTS

25 g (1 oz) creamed coconut,
  chopped
150 ml (¼ pint ⅔ cup) boiling water
1 kg (2¼ lb) skinned monkfish
½ teaspoon ground roasted
  cardamom
2.5 cm (1 in) fresh ginger root, finely
  chopped
½ teaspoon ground roasted cumin
¼-½ teaspoon ground chilli
1 shallot, finely chopped
2 cloves garlic, chopped
1 stalk lemon grass, crushed
salt and freshly ground black pepper

METHOD   Preparation time: 10 minutes

Preheat the oven to 180° C (350° F/ gas 4). Put the coconut into a bowl, pour over the water, stir and leave to melt. Remove the membrane from the fish. Cut out the central bone and divide the fish into four pieces. Mix together the cardamom, ginger, cumin and chilli and rub evenly into the fish.

Put half the shallot and 1 clove garlic into an ovenproof dish that is just large enough to hold the fish in a single layer.

Put the fish on top, tuck the lemon grass between the pieces and sprinkle the remaining shallot and garlic on top. Pour over the coconut, cover and bake until the fish flakes when tested with the point of a sharp knife (30-40 minutes).

Serves 4

INGREDIENTS

4 trout, about 225 g (8 oz) each
1 lime
2 teaspoons fennel seeds
olive oil, for brushing
finely chopped green chillies and lime
  slices, for garnish
Sauce:
400 g (14 oz) red peppers
  (capsicums)
55 g (2 oz) fresh red chillies
2 cloves garlic, crushed
2 tablespoons olive oil
6 tablespoons lemon juice
3-4 tablespoons sugar
salt

METHOD

Preparation time: 10 minutes

To make the sauce, chop the peppers (capsicums) and chillies, then purée with the garlic and 2 tablespoons water. Transfer to a saucepan with the oil, lime juice, sugar, salt and 4 tablespoons water. Bring to the boil, then simmer until reduced by almost half. Leave to cool, then check seasonings, lemon juice and sugar.

Meanwhile, cut two or three deep slashes in both sides of each fish. Cut the lime in half and squeeze the juice into the slashes. Sprinkle the fennel seeds into the cavity of each fish. Leave for 30-60 minutes if time allows.

Preheat the grill. Brush the fish with oil and grill for 5 minutes on each side, until the flesh flakes easily when tested with the point of a sharp knife. Serve with the sauce, and garnished with chopped chilli and lime slices.

Serves 4

INGREDIENTS

2 tablespoons oil, preferably sesame
4 cloves garlic, chopped
1 small fresh red chilli, finely
  chopped
1.25 cm (½ in) fresh ginger root,
  finely chopped
4-5 spring onions (scallions), thickly
  sliced, white and green parts
  separated
1½ tablespoons coarsely chopped
  fermented black beans
2 tablespoons Shaohsing wine or
  medium dry sherry
1 tablespoon dark soy sauce
3 tablespoons chicken stock, or water
24-36 large shelled mussels, fresh, or
  frozen and thawed

METHOD

Preparation time: 10 minutes

Heat the frying pan, then add the oil.
When hot, add the garlic, chilli, ginger
and the white part of the spring
onions (scallions).

Fry for 1½ minutes, then stir in the
fermented black beans. Heat for 45
seconds, then add the Shaohsing wine
or sherry.

When the sizzling ceases, add the soy
sauce and stock or water. Bring to
the boil, then simmer for 10 minutes.
Gently stir in the mussels and heat
through. Serve garnished with the
green part of the spring onions.

Serves 4

INGREDIENTS

12 Mediterranean (king) prawns
  (shrimp)
2 tablespoons olive oil
2 tablespoons lime juice
2 cloves garlic, crushed
2 fresh green chillies, finely chopped
1 teaspoon paprika
½ teaspoon turmeric
1 tablespoon finely chopped
  coriander (cilantro)
salt

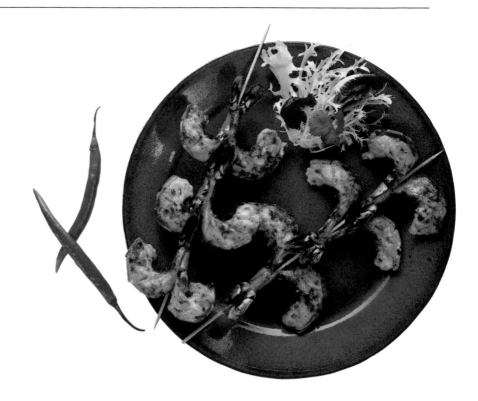

METHOD

Preparation time: 10 minutes

Remove the heads and fine legs from the prawns (shrimp), leaving the tails intact. Using sharp scissors, cut the prawns lengthways almost in half, leaving the tails intact. Put in a shallow, non-metallic dish.

Whisk together the remaining ingredients, pour over the prawns, cover and leave in a cool place, turning occasionally, for 30-60 minutes.

Preheat the grill. Drain the prawns and thread on to four skewers. Grill for 3-4 minutes on each side, basting occasionally with the spice mixture, until just cooked. Serve with any remaining spice mixture.

Serves 4

INGREDIENTS

700 g (1½ lb) cod, haddock or
   monkfish fillets
lemon wedges, to serve
Marinade:
3 tablespoons olive oil
3 cloves garlic, crushed
salt
1½ teaspoons ground roasted cumin
   seeds
1 teaspoon paprika
1 fresh green chilli, finely chopped
handful of coriander (cilantro) leaves,
   finely chopped
juice of 1 lemon

METHOD

Preparation time: 5 minutes

Place the fish in a shallow non-metallic dish. Mix together the marinade ingredients.

Pour the marinade over the fish, cover and leave in a cool place for 3-4 hours, turning occasionally. Cut the fillet into four pieces.

Preheat the grill. Grill the fish for about 4 minutes on each side, brushing with the marinade occasionally, until the flesh flakes with the point of a sharp knife. Serve warm, garnished with lemon wedges.

Serves 4

INGREDIENTS

32 uncooked, unshelled prawns
  (shrimp), about 900 g (2 lb)
1½-2 stalks lemon grass, finely
  chopped
4 tablespoons fish sauce
4 tablespoons lime juice
1 tablespoon finely chopped garlic
3 fresh red chillies, finely chopped
25 g (1 oz) spring onions (scallions),
  white part only, sliced
about 55 g (2 oz) small mint leaves
lettuce leaves, tomato wedges and
  small mint sprigs, to serve

METHOD
Preparation time: 10 minutes

Bring a wide frying pan of water to the boil, add the prawns (shrimp) and bring to simmering point. Drain and leave the prawns until cool enough to handle, then remove the shells, legs and heads. Run the point of a sharp knife along the back of each prawn and remove the dark thread. Leave to cool, but do not chill.

Mix together the lemon grass, fish sauce, lime juice, garlic, chillies, spring onions (scallions) and mint leaves, crushing lightly with the back of a spoon. Toss in the prawns. Taste and add more mint and lemon grass if necessary.

Arrange lettuce leaves on a large serving plate or in a bowl, pile the prawn mixture on top and add tomato wedges and mint sprigs. Serve immediately.

Serves 4 as a main course, 6-8 as a first course

INGREDIENTS

3 fresh green chillies, chopped
2 cloves garlic, chopped
1 teaspoon salt
leaves from large handful of
  coriander (cilantro)
1½ teaspoons roasted cumin seeds
1 tablespoon sugar
2½ tablespoons lime juice
85 g (3 oz) creamed coconut, roughly
  chopped
1 tablespoon boiling water
4 cod steaks, about 175 g (6 oz) each

METHOD

Preparation time: 10 minutes

Put the chillies, garlic, salt, coriander (cilantro), cumin and sugar in a small blender and mix until finely chopped. Add the lime juice, coconut and boiling water and blend to a paste.

Cut four pieces of foil, each large enough to enclose a cod steak. Spread a little coconut mixture in the centre of each piece of foil and place a cod steak on top. Spread with the remaining coconut mixture.

Fold the foil over the fish, folding the edges firmly together to seal. Steam the fish parcels for 20-25 minutes, depending on the thickness of the steaks. Serve the fish in unopened parcels.

Serves 4

– 3 –
POULTRY DISHES

INGREDIENTS

1 tablespoon cumin seeds
1 tablespoon coriander seeds
2.5 cm (1 in) fresh ginger root,
  chopped
½ teaspoon ground turmeric
25 g (1 oz) almonds
2 fresh red chillies, chopped
1 small onion, quartered
3 cloves garlic
350 g (12 oz) red peppers
  (capsicums), seeded and chopped
salt
4 tablespoons groundnut oil
4 chicken breasts
250 ml (8 fl oz/1 cup) water
2 tablespoons lime juice
coriander (cilantro) sprigs to garnish
steamed rice or noodles to serve

METHOD

Preparation time: 20 minutes

Crush the cumin and coriander seeds together using a pestle and mortar, or, alternatively, use the end of a rolling pin in a bowl. Transfer to a food processor and add the ginger, turmeric, almonds, chillies, onion, garlic and peppers (capsicums). Blend until smooth.

Heat the oil in a large, heavy frying pan, add the chicken and cook until brown on both sides. Transfer to a plate. Stir the spice mixture into the pan and cook, while stirring, until the mixture is reduced to a thick paste.

Stir in the water and lime juice. Return the chicken to the pan and turn until thoroughly coated in sauce. Simmer for about 30 minutes until the chicken is tender and the sauce has thickened.

Serves 4

HOT GREEN CHICKEN STRIPS

INGREDIENTS

2 fresh green chillies, chopped
2 cloves garlic
3 coriander (cilantro) sprigs
5 mint sprigs
3 plump spring onions (scallions)
finely grated rind and juice of 1 lime
1 teaspoon caster (superfine) sugar
1 teaspoon Angostura bitters
350 g (12 oz) skinned and boned
*   chicken breasts*
3 tablespoons peanut oil
2 tablespoons cashew nuts
200 ml (7 fl oz/scant 1 cup) chicken
*   stock*
2 teaspoons cornflour (cornstarch)
2 tablespoons soy sauce
boiled rice, to serve

METHOD

Preparation time: 15 minutes

Mix the chillies, garlic, coriander (cilantro), mint, spring onions (scallions), lime rind and juice, sugar, bitters and 3 tablespoons water to a paste in a blender. Arrange the chicken in a single layer, pour over the chilli mixture, cover and leave at room temperature for 2-4 hours.

Remove the chicken from the dish, scraping off the chilli mixture into the dish. Cut the chicken diagonally into thin strips. Heat the oil in a large frying pan, add the chicken and nuts and stir-fry until the chicken turns white. Add the stock and green mixture from the dish, then simmer for 3 minutes.

Mix the cornflour (cornstarch) with the soy sauce to form a paste, then stir into the pan. Cook, stirring, until the mixture thickens. Serve with boiled rice.

Serves 4

METHOD

2 cloves garlic
1 tablespoon chopped ginger root
1½ tablespoons roasted cumin seeds
¾ teaspoon roasted cardamom seeds
150 ml (¼ pint/⅔ cup) thick plain yogurt
½ teaspoon chilli powder
2 teaspoons paprika
salt
8 chicken drumsticks
vegetable oil, for brushing grill rack

METHOD

Preparation time: 5 minutes

With the motor running, drop the garlic and ginger into a blender and chop finely. Switch off the motor, add the cumin and cardamom and blend again briefly. Add the yogurt, chilli, paprika and salt. Mix until evenly blended.

With the point of a sharp knife, cut deep slashes in the chicken, place in a shallow dish and pour over the yogurt mixture; work it into slashes. Cover and leave for 3 hours in a cool place.

Preheat the grill to high heat. Brush the grill rack with oil. Cook the chicken for 3 minutes on each side, basting with the cooking juices when the chicken is turned. Reduce the heat and cook for 6 minutes, turning once and basting with the cooking juices. Serve with the cooking juices spooned over.

Serves 4

INGREDIENTS

2 chickens, each weighing about
   1.25 kg (2½ lb)
juice of 1 lime
salt
2 tablespoons peanut oil
Paste:
8 shallots, chopped
3 cloves garlic
4 fresh red chillies
5 cm (2 in) fresh ginger root
1 teaspoon shrimp or anchovy paste
2 tablespoons peanut oil
juice of 1 lime
4 tomatoes, peeled, seeded and
   chopped
salt

METHOD

Preparation time: 15 minutes

Put the shallots, garlic, chillies, ginger, shrimp or anchovy paste, oil and lime juice into a blender. Blend until smooth. Pour into a saucepan and boil, stirring, for 4 minutes. Add the tomatoes and salt and cook, stirring, for 1-2 minutes. Leave to cool.

Rub the chickens with the paste, inserting it between skin and flesh as well. Enclose each chicken in a large piece of foil, fold the foil over loosely and seal the edges securely. If time allows, leave at room temperature for up to 2 hours, or refrigerate overnight.

Preheat the oven to 180° C (350° F/ gas 4). Cook chicken in oven for 1½ hours. Preheat the grill. Unfold the foil and transfer the chicken to an ovenproof dish. Grill until the skin is browned (about 5 minutes). Pour the juices from the foil into a frying pan, boil until reduced, then serve with the chicken.

Serves 4

INGREDIENTS

2-2.25 kg (4½-5 lb) duck
leaves from a bunch of coriander
  (cilantro)
Paste:
2 cloves garlic
3 fresh green chillies
1 tablespoon roasted coriander seeds
3 fresh bay leaves
2 tablespoons soy sauce
2 tablespoons oyster sauce
2 tablespoons lime juice
1 tablespoon peanut oil
2 tablespoons light brown sugar
5 cm (2 in) fresh ginger root

METHOD

Preparation time: 15 minutes

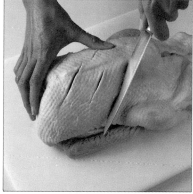

Using a blender, mix the paste ingredients together until as smooth as possible. Remove as much fat as possible from the duck, then prick it with a skewer or large needle. Using a sharp knife, cut slashes in the breast. Put 2 spoonfuls of spice mixture in the cavity of the duck.

Spread the duck evenly with the remaining paste, making sure it goes into slashes. Place on a rack in a shallow baking dish, cover loosely with foil and leave at room temperature for 2 hours, or refrigerate overnight. Preheat oven to 180° C (350° F/gas 4). Remove the foil and roast the duck for about 2¼-2½ hours, basting frequently. Transfer the duck to a warmed plate. Pour the cooking juices into a pan.

Remove the duck flesh from the bones and pile the flesh on a warmed plate. Cover and keep warm. Remove the fat from the cooking juices and boil the juices hard until well reduced and thickened. Pour over the duck and scatter coriander (cilantro) leaves on top.

Serves 4

INGREDIENTS

700 g (1½ lb) chicken joints, cut into
  5 cm (2 in) pieces
4 tablespoons Shaoxing wine, or
  medium sherry
2 teaspoons clear honey
1¼ teaspoons grated fresh ginger root
½ teaspoon freshly ground cinnamon
¾ teaspoon finely crushed coriander
  seeds
pinch of Chinese five-spice powder
pinch of Sichuan pepper
2 tablespoons grated orange rind
1 tablespoon sesame oil
2 spring onions (scallions), thinly sliced
bunch of coriander (cilantro)
vegetable oil, for deep frying
spring onions (scallions), sliced
  diagonally, and coriander (cilantro)
  leaves, to garnish

METHOD   Preparation time: 10 minutes

Put the chicken into a dish. Mix
together half of the wine or sherry
and the honey then mix with the
chicken. Sprinkle with the spices and
orange rind and stir together. Blend
the remaining wine with the sesame
oil, stir into the bowl with the spring
onions (scallions). Cover and leave to
marinate in the refrigerator overnight.

Return the chicken to room
temperature. Cut a 20 cm (8 in)
square of greaseproof paper for each
piece of chicken. Place a sprig of
coriander (cilantro) on each piece of
chicken and loosely wrap in the
greaseproof paper. Seal the edges of
the paper securely.

Half-fill a deep-fat fryer with oil and
heat to 180° C (350° F). Lower in
parcels and cook for 8-10 minutes.
Remove using a slotted spoon.

Serves 4

INGREDIENTS

½ teaspoon saffron threads, crushed
2 tablespoons hot milk
55 g (2 oz/¼ cup) unsalted butter
6 chicken portions, halved
salt and freshly ground black pepper
10 cardamom pods, crushed
10 cloves
2 cinnamon sticks
3 bay leaves
4 cm (1½ in) fresh ginger root, finely
  chopped
55 g (2 oz) slivered almonds
300 ml (10 fl oz/1¼ cups thick plain
  yogurt
1½ teaspoons ground cumin seeds
1½ teaspoons ground coriander
  seeds
½ teaspoon cayenne pepper

METHOD

Preparation time: 30 minutes

Preheat the oven to 180° C/350° F/ gas 4). Leave the saffron threads to infuse in the milk. Heat the butter in a large, non-stick frying pan, add as many chicken portions as will fit in a single layer, sprinkle with salt and pepper and fry until the chicken is lightly browned on both sides. Using tongs, transfer the chicken to a large, ovenproof dish. Fry the remaining chicken in the same way.

Add the cardamom, cloves, cinnamon, bay leaves and ginger to the frying pan and cook, shaking the pan occasionally until the aroma rises. Transfer to the ovenproof dish.

Add the almonds to the frying pan, and fry until they turn an even, medium brown. Pour the contents of the frying pan into the dish.

SAFFRON

Saffron can be used to give a wonderful flavour, aroma and colour to a great variety of dishes. Use it in sauces, rice dishes, soups and many fish and shellfish recipes. Genuine saffron is expensive, as it is produced in limited quantities, but there is no real substitute. Fortunately only small amounts are normally required.

It can be bought as 'threads' or ground powder. Threads are preferable, as powder can be easily adulterated and may not give the flavour you require.

Put the yogurt into a bowl and beat in the cumin, coriander, cayenne, saffron milk and salt and pepper.

Pour over the chicken, cover the dish with foil and bake for 20 minutes. Turn the chicken over, baste with the cooking juices and cook uncovered for about 10 minutes. Transfer the chicken to a warm serving dish. Discard any whole spices that can be easily removed, and pour the sauce over the chicken.

Serves 6

Above: saffron threads and saffron milk

Left: saffron, nuts and spices give this dish its unique flavour

INGREDIENTS

700 g (1½ lb) chicken thighs
1½ tablespoons peanut oil
Sauce:
1 teaspoon roasted Sichuan
  peppercorns, ground
4 teaspoons finely chopped spring
  onions (scallions)
1 clove garlic, finely chopped
2 teaspoons grated ginger
1-1¼ teaspoons shrimp paste
2 fresh red chillies, chopped
1½ teaspoons rice wine or dry sherry
1¼ teaspoons dark soy sauce
few drops of sesame oil

METHOD

Preparation time: 10 minutes

Cut the chicken into 7.5 x 2.5 cm (3 x 1 in) strips.

Heat the peanut oil in a large frying pan or wok. Add the chicken and stir-fry for about 3 minutes. Add all the sauce ingredients except the sesame oil, and continue to stir-fry for a further 3 minutes.

Sprinkle the chicken with sesame oil and serve immediately.

Serves 3-4

INGREDIENTS

3-4 garlic cloves
about 85 g (3 oz) fresh ginger root,
  coarsely chopped
125 ml (4 fl oz/½ cup) hoisin sauce
2 tablespoons soy sauce
1½-2 tablespoons sugar
8 large chicken drumsticks

METHOD
Preparation time: 10 minutes

With the motor running, drop the garlic and ginger into a blender and chop finely. Add the hoisin sauce, soy sauce, sugar and 4 tablespoons water. Mix until smooth.

With the point of a sharp knife, cut four or five slashes in each drumstick. Place in a shallow heatproof dish. Pour over the ginger mixture, making sure it goes into the slashes. Turn the chicken to coat, then cover and refrigerate for 8 hours, turning the chicken occasionally.

Return the chicken to room temperature 30 minutes before cooking. Preheat the grill. Grill the chicken, turning occasionally, for about 25 minutes until the juices run clear when pierced with the point of a sharp knife.

Serves 4

INGREDIENTS

3 cloves garlic
salt
*1½ teaspoons finely crushed black
    pepper*
1½ tablespoons paprika
½ teaspoon cayenne pepper
*1 tablespoon roasted cumin seeds,
    finely crushed*
1 tablespoon turmeric
6 tablespoons lime juice
8 chicken wings
3 tablespoons vegetable oil

METHOD

Preparation time: 5 minutes

Crush the garlic with a little salt to make a paste. Mix with the pepper, paprika, cayenne, cumin, turmeric and lime juice.

Spread the spice mixture over the chicken wings and rub in. Cover and leave at room temperature for 3 hours, or in the refrigerator overnight.

If refrigerated, transfer the chicken to room temperature 30 minutes before cooking. Preheat the grill to high. Brush the grill rack with oil. Cook the chicken wings for 3 minutes on each side, reduce the heat to moderate and cook, basting occasionally with cooking juices, for about 3½ minutes. Transfer to a warmed plate. Pour the cooking juices into a small saucepan, boil until reduced and pour over the chicken wings.

Serves 4

INGREDIENTS

8 chicken thighs
1 tablespoon chopped garlic
1¼ teaspoons finely chopped ginger
  root
2 tablespoons Dijon mustard
2 tablespoons sesame oil
2 tablespoons orange juice
1 tablespoon soy sauce
pinch of chilli powder
coarse salt and freshly ground black
  pepper

METHOD

Preparation time: 5 minutes

Using the point of a sharp knife, cut two or three deep slashes in both sides of each chicken thigh. Arrange as a single layer in a shallow heatproof dish.

Stir together the garlic, ginger, mustard, sesame oil, orange juice, soy sauce, chilli powder, salt and pepper. Spread over the chicken, making sure the mixture goes into the slashes. Cover and leave in a cool place for 2-3 hours, turning the chicken two or three times.

Preheat the grill. Grill chicken thighs, turning occasionally, for about 25 minutes until the juices run clear when pierced with the point of a sharp knife.

Serves 4

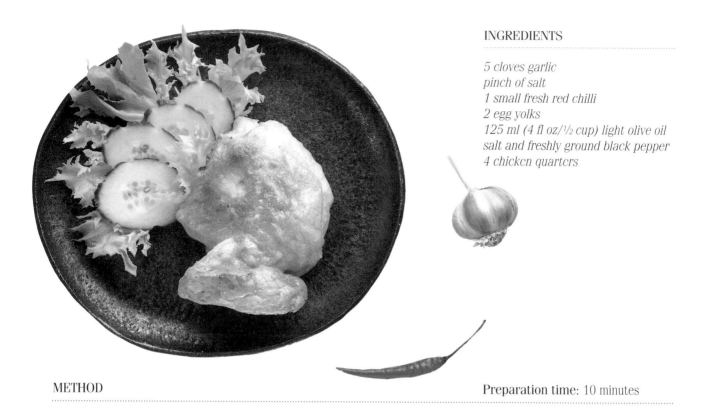

INGREDIENTS

5 cloves garlic
pinch of salt
1 small fresh red chilli
2 egg yolks
125 ml (4 fl oz/½ cup) light olive oil
salt and freshly ground black pepper
4 chicken quarters

METHOD   Preparation time: 10 minutes

Crush the garlic in a mortar with salt and chilli to a paste. Transfer the paste to a bowl and beat in the egg yolks. Beat in the oil drop by drop until the sauce starts to thicken, then add in a slow, steady stream, whisking constantly, to make a mayonnaise-like consistency. Add salt and pepper to taste.

Using your fingers, ease the chicken skin away from the flesh. Using a spoon handle, insert the chilli sauce between skin and flesh. Spread the remaining sauce over the skin. Leave in a cool place for up to 2 hours, if liked.

Preheat the grill. Grill the chicken for 12-15 minutes on each side until the juices run clear when the thickest part of the flesh is pierced with a sharp knife.

Serves 4

- 4 -
MEAT DISHES

INGREDIENTS

*700 g (1½ lb) sirloin steak, cut into
  2.5 cm (1 in) cubes*
*2 teaspoons green chilli, very finely
  chopped*
1 clove garlic, crushed
2 teaspoons grated ginger
4 tablespoons double (heavy) cream
salt
*85 g (3 oz/¾ cup) dried
  breadcrumbs*
1 large egg, beaten
vegetable oil, for frying

METHOD   Preparation time: 10 minutes

Put the steak into a bowl. Stir together the chilli, garlic, ginger and cream. Pour over the steak, stir, then cover and leave in the refrigerator for 3-30 hours.

Put the breadcrumbs in a shallow dish. Dip a few cubes of meat at a time into the egg, allow the excess to drain off, then roll in the breadcrumbs to coat evenly.

Heat a 2.5 cm (1 in) layer of oil in a frying pan over a medium heat. Add the beef in batches so that the pan is never crowded and fry, turning occasionally, until golden and crisp on the outside and cooked to taste inside. Using a slotted spoon, transfer to paper towels to drain. Serve hot.

Serves 4

INGREDIENTS

675 g (1½ lb) rump or sirloin steak
125 ml (4 fl oz/½ cup) peanut oil
Marinade:
2 tablespoons sesame seeds
2 shallots, chopped
3 cloves garlic, chopped
2 small dried red chillies, split
2.5 cm (1 in) fresh ginger root
½ teaspoon sugar
1 tablespoon light soy sauce
2 tablespoons groundnut or olive oil
Sauce:
1 tablespoon tomato purée (paste)
1½ tablespoons mirin or dry sherry
1½ tablespoons light soy sauce
large pinch of chilli powder

METHOD

Preparation time: 20 minutes

Put all the marinade ingredients into a blender and mix until smooth. Transfer to a non-metallic dish. Cut the beef across the grain into wafer-thin slices. Turn them in the marinade to coat evenly, then cover and leave in the refrigerator overnight.

Bring the dish of marinade and beef to room temperature for 30 minutes before cooking. Heat the peanut oil in a wok or large frying pan, add half of the beef and fry briskly for 2 minutes. Transfer to a colander. Cook the remaining beef in the same way. Drain the oil from the wok or pan.

Mix the sauce ingredients in the wok or pan, heat for 1 minute, then add the beef and stir until hot, but for no longer than 2 minutes. Serve immediately.

Serves 4

INGREDIENTS

1½ teaspoons green peppercorns
1 teaspoon black peppercorns
1 teaspoon white peppercorns
4 rump steaks, about 175 g (6 oz)
 each
1 tablespoon olive oil
40 g (1½ oz/1½ tablespoons)
 unsalted butter
few drops of Tabasco sauce
few drops of Worcestershire sauce
2 tablespoons brandy
3 tablespoons double (heavy) cream
salt

METHOD

Preparation time: 10 minutes

Crush the peppercorns together coarsely and press evenly into both sides of each steak. Heat the oil and 15 g (½ oz/½ tablespoon) of the butter in a large frying pan. Add the steaks and cook for 2-3 minutes on each side, or to taste.

Turn the steaks over. Place a quarter of the remaining butter in a piece on each one. Sprinkle with the Tabasco and Worcestershire sauces. Pour over the brandy, then set alight using a lighted taper. When the flames subside, transfer the steaks to a warmed plate.

Stir the cream into the pan, scraping up the sediment and simmer for 1 minute. Add a pinch of salt and pour over the steaks.

Serves 4

SPICY BEEF CASSEROLE

INGREDIENTS

2 tablespoons vegetable oil
1.1 kg (2½ lb) chuck steak, cubed
450 g (1 lb) onions, sliced
225 g (8 oz) button mushrooms
2 cloves garlic, crushed
½ teaspoon ground ginger
1½ teaspoons Curry Powder (see
  page 9)
2 tablespoons plain (all-purpose)
  flour
1 teaspoon dark brown sugar
600 ml (1 pint/2½ cups) brown veal
  stock
2 tablespoons Worcestershire sauce
salt and freshly ground black pepper
2-3 tablespoons creamed horseradish
3 tablespoons chopped parsley

METHOD

Preparation time: 20 minutes

Preheat the oven to 170° C (325° F/ gas 3). Heat the oil in a large flameproof casserole, add the beef in batches and cook quite quickly on the hob (burner) until evenly browned. Using a slotted spoon, transfer to paper towels to drain. Reduce the heat, add the onions, mushrooms and garlic to the casserole and cook for about 4 minutes, stirring occasionally.

Stir in the spices, flour and sugar for 1-2 minutes, then slowly pour in the stock, stirring and bring to the boil, still stirring. Add the beef, Worcestershire sauce and seasonings, cover tightly and place in the oven for about 2 hours, until the beef is very tender.

Stir in the horseradish to taste, sprinkle with the parsley and serve.

Serves 6

INGREDIENTS

450 g (1 lb) rump or sirloin steak
1½ teaspoons sesame oil
2 teaspoons rice wine or dry sherry
1½ teaspoons light soy sauce
1½ teaspoons cornflour (cornstarch)
1 egg white
125 ml (4 fl oz/½ cup) peanut oil
3 fresh red chillies, shredded
10 spring onions (scallions), cut into
  2.5 cm (1 in) pieces
1 small clove garlic, finely chopped
2 teaspoons finely chopped ginger
  root
1½ teaspoons chilli bean sauce
1 teaspoon bean sauce
4 teaspoons oyster sauce

METHOD

Preparation time: 10 minutes

Put the beef into the freezer for 20 minutes, until firm to the touch, then slice very thinly across the grain. Mix together sesame oil, rice wine or sherry, soy sauce, cornflour (cornstarch) and egg white. Add the beef and leave for 20-30 minutes.

Heat a wok until very hot, add the peanut oil and when smoking, add the beef, stirring to separate the slices for 1 minute. Using a slotted spoon, transfer the beef to paper towels. Drain all except 2 tablespoons of oil from the wok.

Add the chillies, spring onions (scallions), garlic, ginger, chilli bean sauce and bean sauce. Stir-fry for 30 seconds, add 2 tablespoons of water and the oyster sauce, simmer for 30 seconds, then return the beef to the wok. Serve sizzling hot.

Serves 4

INGREDIENTS

½ cucumber, diced
1 tablespoon white wine vinegar
salt and freshly ground black pepper
165 g (5½ oz/⅔ cup) Greek yogurt
1 clove garlic, crushed
1 tablespoon chopped mint
450 g (1 lb) lean lamb
115 g (4 oz) pork fat
2 fresh green chillies, finely chopped
1½ teaspoons grated fresh ginger
   root
¾ teaspoon crushed roasted cumin
   seeds
olive oil, for grilling

METHOD

Preparation time: 10 minutes

Put the cucumber into a colander, toss with the vinegar and salt and leave to drain for 1 hour. Rinse and pat dry thoroughly. Mix with the yogurt, garlic, mint and pepper. Cover and refrigerate.

Mince together the lamb and pork fat. Mix in the chillies, ginger, cumin and salt until all the ingredients are thoroughly combined. Divide into 8 portions and roll into thin sausage shapes.

Preheat the grill. Brush the grill rack and sausage shapes with oil and grill them until evenly browned and cooked through (about 3-4 minutes on each side). Serve with cucumber relish.

Serves 4

INGREDIENTS

7 cloves
7 cardamom pods
3 onions, chopped
8 cloves garlic, crushed
5 cm (2 in) fresh ginger root, chopped
3-4 fresh green chillies, chopped
1.3 kg (3 lb) lean lamb
1.3 kg (3 lb) fresh spinach
4 tablespoons mustard oil
7.5 cm (3 in) cinnamon stick
2 bay leaves
2 tablespoons ground roasted
   coriander seeds
1 tablespoon ground roasted cumin
1 teaspoon ground turmeric
1 tomato, peeled, seeded and chopped
2 tablespoons plain yogurt
1 tablespoon Garam Masala (see
   page 8)

METHOD   Preparation time: 20 minutes

Heat a large heavy flameproof casserole, add the cloves and cardamom pods and heat until fragrant. Tip into a blender and add the onions, garlic, ginger, chillies and 5 tablespoons water and blend to a paste. Cut the lamb into 4 cm (1½ in) cubes. Remove the stalks from the spinach and shred the leaves.

Heat the oil in the casserole, add the lamb in batches and cook, stirring occasionally, until browned. Using a slotted spoon, transfer to a bowl. Add the cinnamon and bay leaves to the casserole and cook until the bay leaves darken (10-20 seconds). Stir in the coriander, cumin and spice paste and cook, stirring, until the paste darkens (about 10 minutes); add a few drops of water at a time if the paste sticks.

Stir in the turmeric, tomato and yogurt for 2 minutes before adding the spinach and returning the lamb and any juices in the bowl, to the casserole. Bring to the boil and cover first with foil and then a lid. Cook very gently for 1½ hours, or until the lamb is almost tender, stirring occasionally and adding a little warm water if the meat sticks, but at end of cooking the sauce should be very thick. Stir in the garam masala.

Serves 8

INGREDIENTS

1 teaspoon roasted cumin seeds
1 tablespoon coriander seeds
1 tablespoon wholegrain mustard
1½ tablespoons lime juice
1 tablespoon sesame paste (tahini)
2 cloves garlic, finely chopped
¼-½ teaspoon chilli powder
salt
2 tablespoons olive oil
2 lamb neck fillets, about 350 g (12 oz) each
Chilli dip:
handful of coriander (cilantro) leaves, finely chopped
¼-½ teaspoon chilli powder
salt
150 g (5 oz/⅔ cup) Greek yogurt

METHOD

Preparation time: 5 minutes

Crush together the cumin and coriander seeds. Mix with the mustard, lime juice, sesame paste (tahini), garlic, chilli powder and salt, then slowly pour in the oil, stirring. Put the lamb into a shallow dish and spread evenly with the spicy mixture. Cover and leave at room temperature for 2 hours, or refrigerate overnight.

On the day of serving, stir together the dip ingredients. Cover and chill lightly.

If the lamb has been refrigerated, return to room temperature 30-40 minutes before cooking. Preheat the grill. When the grill is very hot, cook the lamb until blackened in patches (5-8 minutes on each side). Turn off the grill and leave the lamb to rest for about 5 minutes. Serve thickly sliced with the dip.

Serves 4

INGREDIENTS

2 tablespoons finely chopped basil
2 tablespoons finely chopped garlic
2 tablespoons grated ginger root
2 tablespoons finely chopped fresh
  green chillies
2 tablespoons soy sauce
4 pork chops

METHOD   Preparation time: 5 minutes

Using a pestle and mortar or small blender, mix the basil, garlic, ginger and chillies to a paste. Stir in the soy sauce.

Rub the spice mixture into the pork, place in a shallow non-metallic dish, cover and leave at room temperature for 1 hour, or in a cool place for 3 hours.

Preheat the grill. Grill the pork chops for 8-10 minutes on each side, basting with the cooking juices occasionally.

Serves 4

INGREDIENTS

*1.4 kg (3 lb) boned, rolled and tied
    pork loin*
2-3 teaspoons black pepper
1½ teaspoons white pepper
*1½ tablespoons Sichuan
    peppercorns, ground*
1½ tablespoons green peppercorns
¾ teaspoon ground cinnamon
scant ½ teaspoon ground cloves
*2 teaspoons finely crushed fennel
    seeds*
scant ½ teaspoon turmeric
salt
1½ tablespoons sesame oil
3 tablespoons peanut oil
1½ tablespoons grated lemon zest
2 tablespoons grated orange zest
*coriander (cilantro) leaves, to
    garnish*

METHOD

Preparation time: 5 minutes

Put the pork into a shallow, non-metallic dish. Mix together the peppers, peppercorns, cinnamon, cloves, fennel seeds, turmeric and salt. Rub evenly into the pork, cover and leave in a cool place for at least 4 hours, or refrigerate overnight. In a blender, combine the sesame oil, peanut oil and lemon and orange zests. Set aside.

If the pork has been refrigerated, return to room temperature 30 minutes before cooking. Rub the pork with the oil mixture.

Preheat the oven to 180° C (350° F/gas 4). Roast the pork for about 1¼ hours, turning every 10 minutes or so and basting with any cooking juices and remaining oil mixture, until a skewer inserted in the centre comes out clean. Leave to stand for 20 minutes before slicing. Spoon the cooking juices over the slices and garnish with coriander (cilantro) leaves.

Serves 6-8

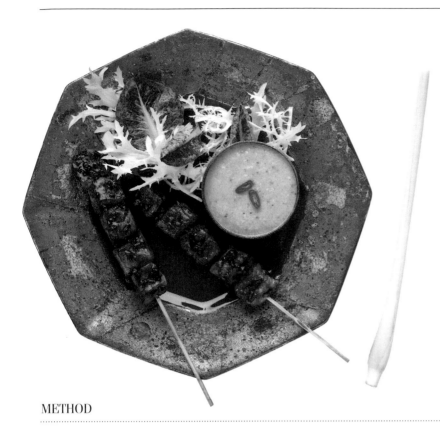

INGREDIENTS

575 g (1¼ lb) lean pork, cut into
  1.25 cm (½ in) cubes
1 small onion, finely chopped
3 tablespoons dark soy sauce
1 teaspoon dark muscovado sugar
salad leaves to serve
Sauce:
4 tablespoons peanut oil
85 g (3 oz) peanuts
2 fresh red chillies, chopped
3 shallots, chopped
2 stalks lemon grass
2 cloves garlic, chopped
2.5 cm (1 in) piece blachan
300 ml (½ pint/1¼ cups) coconut
  milk
2 teaspoons dark muscovado sugar
juice of ½ lime

METHOD

Preparation time: 10 minutes

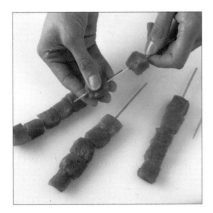

Thread the pork on to eight wooden skewers and lay in a shallow dish. Mix together the onion, soy sauce and sugar, pour over the pork, turning the meat to coat evenly. Cover the dish and leave for at least 1 hour.

For the sauce, heat 1 tablespoon oil over a high heat, add the peanuts and fry, stirring, for 2 minutes. Transfer to paper towels to drain.

Using a pestle and mortar or small blender, mix the chillies, shallots, lemon grass, garlic and blachan to a paste.

Heat the remaining oil over a moderate heat, add the spice paste and fry, stirring for 2 minutes. Grind the nuts until smooth and stir into the paste.

Gradually stir in the coconut milk and bring to the boil. Add the sugar and lime juice and simmer for 5-10 minutes, until thickened. Cover and keep warm over a very low heat.

Preheat the grill. Grill the pork for 4-5 minutes on each side. Place on a bed of salad leaves, and serve with sauce.

Serves 4-5

BLACHAN

When cooked, blachan, a South-east Asian paste made from pounded salted and dried shrimps adds a delicious savoury flavour to dishes. Blachan can be bought from Asian food shops. Substitute anchovy paste, such as Gentleman's Relish, to taste, if unavailable.

Left: small cubes of pork threaded on to wooden skewers have been transferred to a serving plate and presented on a bed of salad leaves.

INGREDIENTS

2 tablespoons vegetable oil
1 onion, chopped
575 g (1¼ lb) lean veal, cut into
  2.5 cm (1 in) cubes
1½ tablespoons seasoned flour
1 teaspoon black peppercorns,
  crushed
1 heaped tablespoon Hungarian
  paprika
¼ teaspoon cayenne pepper, or to
  taste
1¼ teaspoons roasted cumin seeds
5 cm (2 in) cinnamon stick
400 g (14 oz) can chopped Italian
  tomatoes
1 red pepper (capsicum), seeded and
  chopped
150 ml (¼ pint/⅔ cup) soured
  cream, and paprika, to serve

METHOD

Preparation time: 10 minutes

Heat the oil in a large saucepan or heavy flameproof casserole, add the onion and cook over a medium heat until softened but not coloured (about 4 minutes).

Meanwhile, toss the veal in the flour. Add to the casserole and fry until sealed. Reduce the heat and stir in the peppercorns, paprika, cayenne, cumin, cinnamon, tomatoes and red pepper.

Bring just to simmering point, then simmer very gently, uncovered, until the veal is tender and liquid thickened (about 1¼ hours). Discard the cinnamon. Top each serving with a spoonful of soured cream and a very fine dusting of paprika.

Serves 4

– 5 –
VEGETABLES, RICE
AND NOODLES

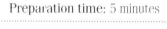

INGREDIENTS

350 g (12 oz) oyster, or medium cap, mushrooms
4 tablespoons olive oil
3 cloves garlic, chopped
2.5 cm (1 in) fresh ginger root, finely chopped
1 teaspoon lightly crushed Sichuan peppercorns
1 tablespoon sesame seeds

METHOD

Preparation time: 5 minutes

Break the mushrooms into large pieces. Heat the oil in a frying pan, add the garlic, ginger and peppercorns.

Cook for 1-2 minutes, then stir in the mushrooms. Cook for 4-5 minutes, stirring occasionally.

Stir in the sesame seeds for about 30 seconds. Serve immediately.

Serves 4

CHILLI POTATOES

INGREDIENTS

1 kg (2¼ lb) waxy potatoes
salt
4 tablespoons vegetable oil
1 teaspoon black mustard seeds
1 onion, thinly sliced
2 large cloves garlic, finely crushed
2 bay leaves
2 dried chillies
1 teaspoon ground cumin
½ teaspoon turmeric
2 long fresh green chillies, finely
   shredded

METHOD

Preparation time: 15 minutes

Cut the potatoes into 2 cm (¾ in) chunks and add to a saucepan of boiling, salted water. Boil for 4 minutes, then drain well.

Heat the oil in a large saucepan, add the mustard seeds and cook for about 30 seconds until they pop. Add the onion and cook, stirring occasionally, for about 4 minutes, or until tender. Add the garlic, bay leaves, dried chillies, cumin and turmeric. Cook for about 1 minute, then stir in the potatoes. Add 3 tablespoons water, cover and cook over a very low heat for about 5 minutes.

Add the fresh chillies to the pan, cover again and continue cooking until the potatoes are tender and there is no more liquid (about 10 minutes).

Serves 4

INGREDIENTS

450 g (1 lb) fresh spinach
1 tablespoon peanut oil
1 clove garlic, finely crushed
1 fresh green chilli, chopped
1 fresh red chilli, chopped
1 teaspoon finely chopped fresh
  ginger root
oyster sauce

METHOD

Preparation time: 10 minutes

Remove the stalks from the spinach and tear the leaves into large pieces. Add to a large saucepan of boiling water and blanch for 45 seconds.

Drain the spinach and rinse immediately under cold running water, then squeeze hard in a colander until completely dry.

Heat a wok over a high heat until very hot, add the oil and heat until smoking. Add the garlic, chillies and ginger. Toss for a few seconds, then add the spinach rapidly, tossing quickly to separate pieces and coat with oil. Sprinkle with a little oyster sauce, toss and serve immediately.

Serves 2

INGREDIENTS

85 g (3 oz/¾ cup) walnut halves
*150 ml (¼ pint/⅔ cup) double
  (heavy) cream*
*2-3 tablespoons hot horseradish
  cream*
*1 tablespoon finely chopped fresh
  ginger root*
salt
lemon juice
sugar (optional)
about 450 g (1 lb) cooked beetroot

METHOD

Preparation time: 5 minutes

If time allows, pour boiling water over the walnuts in batches, leave for 2 minutes, then remove using a slotted spoon and scrape off the skins using a small, sharp knife.

Chop the walnuts. Stir into the cream with the horseradish, ginger, salt and lemon juice to taste, until evenly blended. Add a pinch of sugar, if liked.

Peel the beetroot and cut into dice. Pile into a shallow serving bowl, spoon on a little of the sauce and serve the rest separately.

Serves 4

INGREDIENTS

150 g (5 oz/¾ cup) split peas
½ teaspoon turmeric
1 tablespoon finely chopped fresh
  ginger root
1 clove garlic, crushed
2 fresh green chillies, finely chopped
350 g (12 oz) tomatoes
350 g (12 oz) aubergines (eggplants)
2 courgettes (zucchini)
½ small cauliflower
4 tablespoons peanut oil
1 teaspoon black mustard seeds
1 teaspoon cumin seeds
1 small onion, thinly sliced
pinch of freshly ground asafetida
  (optional)
salt
chopped coriander (cilantro), to
  serve

METHOD   Preparation time: 20 minutes

Boil the split peas with 750 ml (24 fl oz/3 cups) water, the turmeric, ginger, garlic and chillies until tender and the liquid absorbed (1½-2 hours).

Meanwhile, peel, seed and chop the tomatoes. Cut the aubergines (eggplants) and courgettes (zucchini) into sticks about 4 cm (1½ in) long. Break the cauliflower into florets.

Heat the oil, add the mustard seeds and heat until the splattering stops. Add the cumin, heat for 5-10 seconds, then stir in the asafetida and onion and cook over a high heat for 1 minute.

Add the tomatoes and cook, stirring but without breaking up pieces, for 3-4 minutes. Add the aubergine and cauliflower and cook for 3 minutes.

Stir in the split pea mixture and salt, then simmer, covered, for 10-15 minutes.

Add the courgettes, cover and continue cooking until the vegetables are tender (about 10 minutes more). Serve sprinkled with coriander (cilantro).

Serves 4-6

ASAFETIDA

Asafetida has a distinctive pungent smell before cooking, but afterwards develops a taste similar to that of onions. It can be bought from Indian food shops, but if it is unavailable it can be omitted.

Left: A combination of fresh vegetables and split peas form the basis of this curry. Traditional spices and flavourings create the distinctive curry taste.

INGREDIENTS

4 tablespoons vegetable oil
1 teaspoon cumin seeds
2 fresh green chillies, chopped
1.25 cm (½ in) fresh ginger root,
* finely chopped*
2½ tablespoons coriander seeds,
* crushed*
1 kg (2¼ lb) young carrots, thinly
* sliced*
½ teaspoon ground turmeric
25 g (1 oz) fresh coriander (cilantro),
* very finely chopped*
salt

METHOD

Preparation time: 15 minutes

Heat the oil in a wok or frying pan. Add the cumin seeds, heat until starting to sizzle and then add the chillies and ginger.

When the ginger starts to brown, stir in the coriander seeds, then the carrots and turmeric. Stir for 2 minutes.

Add the chopped coriander (cilantro) and salt, stir once, then cover the pan and simmer for 3-4 minutes, until the carrots are just tender. Using a slotted spoon, transfer the carrots and coriander to a warmed serving dish.

Serves 6

INGREDIENTS

700 g (1½ lb) aubergines (eggplants)
1½ tablespoons peanut oil
Sauce:
1 1/2 teaspoons finely chopped
 ginger
1 clove garlic, finely chopped
1½ teaspoons chilli bean sauce
2 teaspoons rice wine or dry sherry
1 tablespoon finely chopped
 coriander (cilantro)
1 fresh red chilli, finely chopped
3 spring onions (scallions), white
 parts and some green, sliced
 diagonally
1½ teaspoons black rice vinegar
salt and freshly ground black pepper
toasted sesame seeds, to serve

METHOD

Preparation time: 25 minutes

Preheat the oven to 180° C (350° F/ gas 4). Bake the aubergines (eggplants) for 15 minutes. Allow to cool slightly, then peel and using two forks, shred them into long pieces. The skins can be removed, if liked.

Heat a wok or large frying pan, add the oil, heat, then stir in the ginger, garlic and chilli bean sauce. Stir-fry for 30 seconds.

Add the aubergine and remaining sauce ingredients, and cook for 2 minutes. Serve hot or at room temperature sprinkled with toasted sesame seeds.

Serves 3-4

INGREDIENTS

200 g (7 oz/1 cup) basmati rice
2 dried red chillies
1¼ teaspoons black peppercorns
1¼ teaspoons cumin seeds
1 teaspoon coriander seeds
4 black cardamom pods
6 cloves
¾ cinnamon stick
3 tablespoons olive oil
1 bay leaf
3 shallots, chopped
2-3 cloves garlic, chopped
1 fresh green chilli, finely chopped
chopped coriander (cilantro), to
  garnish

METHOD   Preparation time: 25 minutes

Put the rice into a strainer and rinse under cold running water until the water runs clear. Tip the rice into a bowl and soak in 400 ml (14 fl oz/1 ¾ cups) cold water for 30 minutes.

Put the dried chillies and spices into a hot, heavy-based saucepan, and heat for about 1½ minutes, shaking the pan constantly. Tip the contents into a bowl and crush lightly. Add the oil to the pan, heat, then stir in the bay leaf, shallots and garlic. Cook for 4 minutes, stirring occasionally.

Drain the rice and reserve the water. Stir the rice into the pan with the crushed spice mixture and fry for 2-3 minutes until the rice is opaque. Stir in the reserved water, bring to the boil, then cover the pan and simmer for 12-15 minutes, or until liquid is absorbed and rice is tender. Turn off heat and leave for 5 minutes. Fluff up the rice and garnish with fresh chilli and coriander (cilantro).

Serves 4

INGREDIENTS

3 tablespoons vegetable oil
4 cloves garlic, finely crushed
1 fresh red chilli, finely chopped
1 fresh green chilli, finely chopped
1 tablespoon fish sauce
3-4 tablespoons lime juice
1 teaspoon sugar
2 eggs, beaten
350 g (12 oz) rice vermicelli, soaked
  in water for 20 minutes, drained
150 g (5 oz) cooked shelled shrimps
115 g (4 oz) beansprouts
4 spring onions (scallions), sliced
2 tablespoons chopped coriander
  (cilantro)
finely chopped roasted peanuts,
  coriander (cilantro) leaves and lime
  slices, to garnish

METHOD

Preparation time: 10 minutes

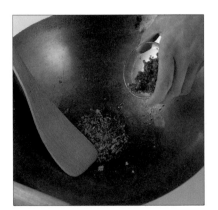

Heat the oil in a wok or large frying pan, add the garlic and cook, stirring occasionally, until it starts to turn golden. Stir in the chillies and cook for 1-2 minutes. Stir in the fish sauce, lime juice and sugar until the sugar has dissolved.

Stir in the eggs quickly and cook for a few seconds. Stir in the noodles until well coated, then add 85 g (3 oz) of the shrimps and 85 g (3 oz) of the beansprouts, half the spring onions (scallions) and coriander (cilantro).

When the noodles are tender, transfer the contents of the wok or pan to a serving dish and garnish with the remaining shrimps, beansprouts and spring onions, peanuts, coriander leaves and lime slices.

Serves 4

INGREDIENTS

2 tablespoons vegetable oil
1 onion, finely chopped
4 cloves garlic, finely chopped
2 teaspoons crushed coriander seeds
2½ teaspoons crushed cumin seeds
¼ teaspoon cayenne pepper
*½ teaspoon Garam Masala (see
  page 8)*
1 teaspoon paprika
¼ teaspoon turmeric
350 g (12 oz) cooked chick-peas
1 tablespoon tomato purée (paste)
150 ml (5 fl oz/⅔ cup) water
salt
1-1½ tablespoons lemon juice
1 teaspoon grated fresh ginger root
1 fresh green chilli, finely chopped

METHOD

Preparation time: 10 minutes

Heat the oil in a saucepan, add the onion and garlic and fry for about 4 minutes, stirring occasionally, until softened. Stir in the coriander, cumin, cayenne, garam masala, paprika and turmeric for a few seconds.

Add the chick-peas and cook, stirring occasionally, until lightly browned.

Stir in the tomato purée (paste), water, salt and lemon juice. Cover and simmer gently for 10 minutes. Stir in the ginger and chilli and cook for 30 seconds.

Serves 4

INGREDIENTS

350 g (12 oz) white haricot beans
2 tablespoons vegetable oil
1 onion, chopped
2 cloves garlic, chopped
3 fresh red chillies, chopped
700 g (1½ lb) tomatoes, peeled and
* chopped*
600 ml (1 pint/2½ cups) vegetable
* stock, or water*
2 teaspoons English mustard powder
1 tablespoon grain mustard
3 tablespoons molasses or black
* treacle*
1½ tablespoons Worcestershire
* sauce*
1 tablespoon paprika
sprig of thyme
115 g (4 oz) piece bacon
salt and freshly ground black pepper

METHOD

Preparation time: 10 minutes

Soak the beans in plenty of cold water overnight, then drain. Heat the oil in a heavy flameproof casserole, add the onion and garlic and cook gently, stirring occasionally, until the onion begins to soften. Stir in the chillies and cook for 2-3 minutes.

Stir in the remaining ingredients, placing the bacon in the middle. Bring to the boil and then simmer, uncovered, for 15 minutes.

Preheat the oven to 180° C (350° F/ gas 4). Cover the casserole and cook in the oven until the beans are tender (about 2 hours). Check the flavourings and seasoning and chop the bacon before serving.

Serves 4

INGREDIENTS

175 g (6 oz/¾ cup) Thai jasmine rice
115 g (4 oz) French (green) beans,
  cut into 2.5 cm (1 in) lengths
2 tablespoons vegetable oil
1 large onion, finely chopped
3 cloves garlic, chopped
1 fresh green chilli, finely chopped
2 tablespoons Nam Prik, (see
  page 10)
85 g (3 oz) chicken, diced
2 eggs, beaten
1 tablespoon fish sauce
55 g (2 oz/⅓ cup) cooked shelled
  prawns (shrimp)
finely sliced red chilli, shredded
  coriander (cilantro) leaves and
  diagonally sliced spring onions
  (scallions), for garnish

METHOD   **Preparation time:** 20 minutes

Rinse the rice several times under cold running water. Put into a heavy saucepan with 300 ml (½ pint/1¼ cups) water, cover and bring to the boil quickly.

Uncover and stir vigorously until the water has evaporated. Reduce the heat to very low, cover the pan tightly first with foil, then with the lid. Leave the rice to steam for 20 minutes until tender, light, fluffy and every grain is separated.

Add the beans to a saucepan of boiling water and boil for 2 minutes. Drain and refresh under cold running water. Drain well.

Heat the oil in a wok, add the onion, garlic and chillies and cook, stirring occasionally, until the onion has softened. Stir in the nam prik and continue to stir for 3-4 minutes.

Add the chicken and stir-fry for 2 minutes. Stir in the rice until it is well coated, then push to the sides of the wok. Pour the eggs into the centre of the wok. When just beginning to set, mix evenly into the rice, adding the fish sauce at the same time.

Stir in the prawns (shrimp), then transfer to a shallow, warmed serving dish and garnish with chilli, coriander (cilantro) and spring onions (scallions).

Serves 4

JASMINE RICE

Thai jasmine rice is a long-grain white rice with an attractive fragrance, hence its alternative name of 'Thai fragrant rice'. When cooked it has a slightly more sticky texture than basmati rice. Highly prized in South-east Asia, it is now becoming more readily available in Western supermarkets.

Left: If you are using a single serving bowl, try garnishing the dish with a decorative spring onion (scallion) flower.

INGREDIENTS

400 g (14 oz) bucatini
salt
125 ml (4 fl oz/½ cup) olive oil
6 dried red chillies
4 cloves garlic

METHOD   Preparation time: 10 minutes

Bring a large saucepan of salted water to the boil, add the bucatini, stir, cover and return to the boil. Uncover and simmer for 10-12 minutes, until the pasta is tender but still firm to the bite. Drain.

Meanwhile, pour half the oil into a frying pan, add the chillies and 3 garlic cloves. Stir over a medium heat until the chillies have become shiny and swollen, but do not allow either the chillies or garlic to burn. Transfer to a small blender and mix to a paste. Add the remaining oil to the pan, heat, then add the remaining garlic and heat until brown. Stir in the paste and simmer for 5 minutes, stirring.

Tip the pasta into a warm serving bowl. Discard the whole garlic from the sauce, add salt to taste and pour over the pasta, toss well and serve immediately.

Serves 4

INGREDIENTS

225 g (8 oz/2 cups) plain (all-purpose) flour
2 teaspoons baking powder
1 teaspoon bicarbonate of soda
1 teaspoon ground cinnamon
1 teaspoon ground allspice
3½ teaspoons ground ginger
2 tablespoons ground almonds
2 eggs, beaten
115 g (4 oz/½ cup) unsalted butter, diced
2 1/2 tablespoons black treacle
2 tablespoons stem ginger syrup
2 tablespoons dark brown sugar
85 ml (3 fl oz/⅓ cup) soured cream
175 g (6 oz/1 cup) chopped stem ginger
2 tablespoons rum

METHOD

Preparation time: 10 minutes

Preheat the oven to 180° C (350° F/ gas 4). Butter and line a 20 cm (8 in) cake tin. Sift together the flour, baking powder, bicarbonate of soda and spices. Stir in the ground almonds and make a well in the centre. Pour the eggs into the well.

Gently heat the butter, treacle, ginger syrup and sugar in a small saucepan until melted and evenly mixed. Stir in the soured cream, then slowly pour into the well, stirring the dry ingredients into the liquid to make a smooth batter. Add the stem ginger and rum.

Pour into the prepared cake tin and bake until a skewer inserted in the centre comes out clean (45-50 minutes). Leave to cool in the tin. Turn out and wrap in greaseproof (waxed) paper and keep in an airtight container for at least 1-2 days before eating. The cake improves on keeping.

Makes one 20 cm (8 in) cake.

INGREDIENTS

700 g (1½ lb) mixed dried fruit such
   as pears, apricots, figs, peaches
   and apple rings
1 lemon
2 large oranges
seeds from 6 cardamom pods, lightly
   crushed
5 cm (2 in) cinnamon stick
4 star anise pods (optional)
4 cloves
400 ml (14 fl oz/1¾ cups) fruity
   medium dry white wine, such as
   Chenin blanc
300 ml (½ pint/1¼ cups) apple juice
chilled Greek yogurt, to serve

METHOD

Place the dried fruit in a bowl. Using a potato peeler, pare a long strip of rind from the lemon and 1 orange. Squeeze the juice from the lemon and add with the rind and spices to the dried fruit. Pour over the wine, stir, cover and leave in a cool place overnight.

Tip the contents of the bowl into a saucepan, add the apple juice and simmer gently until the fruit is just tender (about 25 minutes). Leave to cool and then chill lightly.

Just before serving, peel the oranges, remove all the skin and pith and divide into segments. Stir into the dried fruit and serve with Greek yogurt.

Serves 6

INGREDIENTS

2 ripe but firm nectarines
2-4 slices of brioche, or other rich,
  firm bread such as cholla, crusts
  removed
about 55 g (2 oz/¼ cup) unsalted
  butter
½ teaspoon coriander seeds
½ teaspoon Sichuan peppercorns
2 cm (¾ in) cinnamon stick
about 55 g (2 oz/¼ cup) light
  muscovado sugar
about 3 tablespoons flaked almonds
cream, ice cream or Greek yogurt, to
  serve

METHOD

Preparation time: 10 minutes

Preheat the oven to 180° C (350° F/ gas 4). Butter a shallow baking tin. Place the nectarines in a bowl, cover with boiling water and leave for about 30 seconds. Remove and peel, then cut each nectarine in half and remove the stone (pit).

Cut the slices of bread in half if large. Butter one side of each slice generously. Crush the spices together very finely. Mix with the sugar and sprinkle some over the bread.

Place a nectarine half, cut-side down, on each piece of bread and cut deep slashes in the fruit. Insert slivers of butter in the slashes, scatter the almonds on top and sprinkle generously with the sugar and spice mixture. Lay the slices on the baking sheet and bake for about 15 minutes until the bread is crisp and browned at edges, the fruit softened and coated in sauce. Serve warm with cream, ice cream or strained Greek yogurt.

Serves 2-4

CARIBBEAN BANANAS

INGREDIENTS

4 large firm bananas
40 g (1½ oz/1½ tablespoons)
  unsalted butter
1 teaspoon finely crushed allspice
  berries, or ground mixed spice
2 tablespoons muscovado sugar
grated rind of ½ orange
juice of 1 large orange
juice of 1 lime
3 tablespoons dark rum
1 tablespoon Cointreau, or other
  orange liqueur

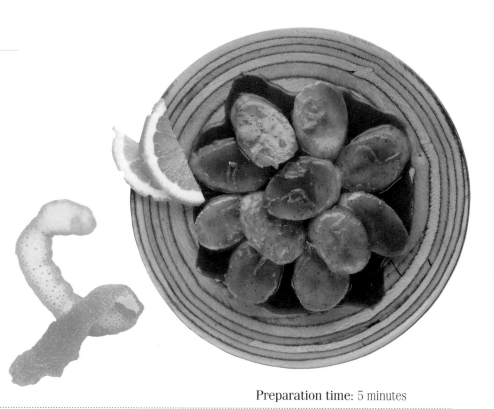

METHOD

Preparation time: 5 minutes

Peel the bananas and cut diagonally into thick slices. Melt the butter in a frying pan, stir in the allspice or mixed spice, then the bananas and fry gently, turning occasionally, until the bananas have softened and are lightly browned. Transfer the bananas to a warmed serving dish.

Stir the sugar into the frying pan until melted. Heat until lightly caramelized, then stir in the orange rind and juice and lime juice. Boil the mixture for a few minutes until slightly thickened. Return the bananas to the pan and remove from the heat.

Heat the rum and liqueur in a ladle over a flame. Ignite the mixture using a lighted taper, then carefully pour into the pan, return to the heat and shake to mix the ingredients. Serve immediately.

Serves 4

INGREDIENTS

10 cloves
1 orange
1 lemon
55 g (2 oz) sugar cubes
2.5 cm (1 in) cinnamon stick
1 blade mace
5 allspice berries, lightly crushed
³/₄ bottle claret
³/₄ bottle port

METHOD   Preparation time: 5 minutes

Preheat the oven to 180° C (350° F/ gas 4). Stud the orange with the cloves, then bake in the oven for 30 minutes. Rub the lemon rind with the sugar cuves and reserve the sugar. Squeeze the lemon juice.

Cut the orange into quarters whilst holding it over a saucepan. Add the orange to the pan with cinnamon, mace, allspice and 175 ml (6 fl oz/³/₄ cup) water. Bring to the boil and simmer for 10 minutes.

Add the sugar cubes, lemon juice, wine and port. Heat gently to just below simmering point, cover and keep warm over a very low heat for 10 minutes. Serve in warmed mugs or glasses.

Serves 8

INGREDIENTS

*1 litre (1³/₄ pints/4¹/₄ cups) fresh hot
  strong coffee*
1 small stick cinnamon
¹/₄ teaspoon freshly grated nutmeg
5 cardamom pods, crushed
caster (superfine) sugar, to taste
*ice cubes, whipped double (heavy)
  cream and chocolate powder, to
  serve*

METHOD

Preparation time: 5 minutes

Pour the hot coffee into a bowl. Add
the cinnamon, nutmeg and
cardamom. Cover, leave to cool, then
refrigerate for at least 4 hours.

Strain the coffee and add sugar to
taste, stirring until it is dissolved.

Pour into tall glasses. Add ice cubes,
top with whipped cream and sprinkle
with chocolate powder.

Makes 1 litre (1³/₄ pints/4¹/₄ cups)